# JUNIOR MARTIAL ARTS
## Concentration

# Junior Martial Arts

All Around Good Habits
Confidence
Concentration
Hand-Eye Coordination
Handling Peer Pressure
Safety
Self-Defense
Self-Discipline
Self-Esteem

## JUNIOR MARTIAL ARTS
# Concentration

### KIM ETINGOFF

MASON CREST

Mason Crest
450 Parkway Drive, Suite D
Broomall, PA 19008
www.masoncrest.com

Printed and bound in the United States of America.

First printing
9 8 7 6 5 4 3 2 1

Series ISBN: 978-1-4222-2731-2
ISBN: 978-1-4222-2733-6
ebook ISBN: 978-1-4222-9066-8

The Library of Congress has cataloged the
hardcopy format(s) as follows:

Library of Congress Cataloging-in-Publication Data

Etingoff, Kim.
  Concentration / Kim Etingoff.
      pages cm. – (Junior martial arts)
    ISBN 978-1-4222-2733-6 (hardcover) – ISBN 978-1-4222-2731-2 (series) – ISBN 978-1-4222-9066-8 (ebook)
  1. Martial arts–Juvenile literature. 2. Attention–Juvenile literature. I. Title.
  GV1101.35.E784 2014
  796.8–dc23
                                   2013004746

Publisher's notes:
The websites mentioned in this book were active at the time of publication. The publisher is not responsible for websites that have changed their addresses or discontinued operation since the date of publication. The publisher will review and update the website addresses each time the book is reprinted.

# Contents

1. More Than Fighting                                    7

2. Concentration and Martial Arts                       13

3. Improving Your Concentration                         19

4. Concentration and Your Life                          25

Words to Know                                           29

Find Out More                                           30

Index                                                   31

About the Author & Picture Credits                      32

# 1

# MORE THAN FIGHTING

Imagine yourself as a martial arts master. What are you doing? Leaping through the air? Punching as fast as you can?

What about doing well on tests at school? Or feeling good about yourself? Or feeling happier? That might not be what you think of when you think about martial arts. But martial arts really can change the way you think and feel!

Martial arts are about more than fighting. Some people think that martial arts are about hurting others. It's true that martial arts can help you **defend** yourself. You learn kicks and punches and other moves. But you aren't supposed to go around and use them every day. Hurting people isn't really the point of martial arts.

Using weapons in karate, hapkido, or other martial arts takes a lot of concentration. Focusing on staying safe is a great way to make sure everyone has fun and learns a lot.

Martial arts are more about what's going on in your head. You have to think about the moves you're doing. There's a lot going on in your mind when you're practicing martial arts.

# What Are Martial Arts?

Martial arts are ways of defending yourself. But every kind of martial art is a little different. Each kind of martial arts has its own moves. Each has its own **traditions**. You don't have to be super strong. You just have to know how to move the right way.

Some martial arts are done standing up. Some are more about being on the ground. Some use fake weapons. Others don't use anything except your own hands and feet. You can see how different they all are!

Each kind of martial art has its own name. And they each have their own history. There are martial arts from Asia. You might know karate and jiu-jitsu from Japan. Taekwondo is from Korea. Other Asian countries from China to Malaysia have their own versions of martial arts, too.

There are also martial arts from other parts of the world. Capoeira is from Brazil. Fencing and boxing are from Europe.

You can **practice** any of these kinds of martial arts all around the world. There are teachers who teach each kind. You don't have to live in Korea to learn taekwondo, or Brazil to learn capoeira.

Some martial arts are very old. They have been around for thousands of years. Others are newer. Martial art teachers come up with new kinds of martial arts all the time.

Have you ever seen actors performing martial arts in a movie? Real martial arts aren't quite like that. Movies make martial arts look exciting. In the movies, martial artists jump over buses or fly through the air. Martial arts almost seem like magic.

Real-life martial arts aren't that magical. But in real life, you'll still get to learn things you thought you'd never be able to do. After a lot of practice, you'll be able to break boards with your hands, or throw people bigger than you to the ground.

Martial arts may be about learning punches and kicks sometimes. But they're not about hurting others with what you learn in class. Martial arts teach you a lot more than fighting.

# Martial Arts and Weapons

The Korean martial art of hapkido sometimes uses weapons. As students learn more, they start learning how to fight with weapons. Hapkido students use knives. They use short sticks and longer sticks. They use rope. Some even use swords. Sometimes two people with weapons fight each other. Sometimes only one person has a weapon. And sometimes people doing hapkido don't have any weapons at all.

Using dangerous weapons takes practice. It also takes concentration. Focusing while using weapons is important for keeping everyone safe.

# Getting Better

Lots of kids and adults do martial arts to become better people. How does that happen? In a lot of ways!

Martial arts are exercise. When we practice them, we can get healthier and more in shape. Moving around a lot and using our bodies is good for us. We'll be stronger and feel better.

Martial arts teach **respect**. Martial art students can learn how to be better friends and students. You'll get along better with your teachers, parents, and friends if you learn how to respect others.

These are just a couple of examples of how martial arts can make your life even better. Martial arts can teach us to be better people in a lot of different ways.

Another way of thinking about it is that martial arts give you all kinds of life **skills**. That means they teach you things that are useful every day. If you study martial arts, you'll learn more than just how to kick and punch.

You'll learn how to concentrate on things. You'll learn how to be calm and feel happier. You might even feel better about yourself and what you can do.

All of the skills you learn will help you in different parts of your life. You'll do better in school. You'll be a better friend. You'll get along better with your family.

But all that takes hard work. You can't just start doing martial arts and become a better person the next day. You have to practice for a long time. If you put in some work, you'll see the changes in yourself. You'll get better and better at martial arts. You might feel better. You can do better in school!

## What Else?

Martial arts teach you a lot of skills. On the outside, your body gets stronger. You get in better shape. Martial arts are a workout! You might build some muscles. Or lose weight if you need to. On the inside, you'll feel better about yourself. You'll also be amazed at everything you can do after you practice martial arts for a while.

# Concentration

One thing martial arts can do for you is give you more concentration. Of course, it doesn't come without a lot of hard work.

Concentration is how well you can focus on something. It could be how well you focus on what your teacher is saying at school. Concentration is paying attention to your homework until it's finished. It could be how well you can focus on doing chores at home.

When you can concentrate on things, you can keep doing them for a long time. You don't get **distracted** by other stuff. When you're focusing on your homework, you get more answers right. When you're doing homework while talking to your friends or watching a movie, you probably won't do as well.

Everyone can use a little help concentrating! There are a lot of things out there in the world that can distract us. Using the computer, watching TV, playing with friends are all fun things to do sometimes. But they also can be distracting when we're trying to concentrate on something.

A lot of the time, we need to concentrate. If you have to do homework or help your mom or dad, you have to be able to pay attention and concentrate.

Why is concentration important? It helps us get things done. It helps us learn. And it helps make us happy.

You might think concentrating at school is boring. But learning is very important! Concentrating on schoolwork will help you get good grades and learn things. And that will help you in the future.

Outside of school, concentrating is important, too. You need a lot of concentration to play games and sports well.

Luckily, we can all get better at concentrating. It's something we can learn. One thing that helps you concentrate is martial arts. By practicing martial arts, you can get better and better at concentrating!

# 2

# CONCENTRATION AND MARTIAL ARTS

oncentration is one of the most important parts of learning martial arts. After all, how are you going to learn how to do martial arts if you aren't paying attention? Martial arts aren't the only way to learn to concentrate, but they are one of the best.

## The Teacher

Your teacher is important when you're learning martial arts. Often, martial arts students call their teacher the "master" or "sensei."

The master is in charge of making sure his students are learning. He shows his students new moves. He teaches them new ways of thinking about things. He gives them tips on how to do things better.

Listening to the teacher is one of the most important parts of learning any martial art. Your teacher wants you to listen, learn, stay safe, and have fun. He has a lot to teach you, so make sure you're always paying attention in class!

14    CONCENTRATION

You need to pay a lot of attention to the teacher. If you don't concentrate on what she's saying, you won't keep up. If you're taking martial arts classes, you probably want to get better at it. You want to keep up with what everyone else is doing. Concentrating on the teacher is a big part of that.

It doesn't have to be hard to concentrate on the teacher. There aren't usually many distractions in the martial arts studio or gym where you're practicing. No one is talking on a cell phone. There aren't computers or TVs around. People aren't talking to each other. Everyone is watching and listening to the teacher.

What the teacher is saying is interesting, too! You want to pay attention, because you'll learn cool new things. Your teacher is the key to being a good martial artist.

## Taekwondo Teachers

Teachers in taekwondo are called Masters or Grandmasters. Grandmasters run the school. They teach the teachers. Both Masters and Grandmasters have studied taekwondo for a long time. They have their black belts, the highest level you can get in taekwondo. They also know how to teach. They have to teach students who have just started. They have to teach students who have practiced taekwondo for years. And they have to teach everyone in between. It can be a lot of work! And all that work takes a lot of concentration!

# You

In martial arts, you also have to concentrate—on you. You need to pay attention to what you're doing. That's another way you'll get better at martial arts.

First, you concentrate on what your teacher tells you to do. Now you have to actually follow his directions. You think really hard about what your arms and legsare doing. Where should your hands be pointing? What should you be looking at?

You probably won't get it right the very first time. When you try a new roll onto the floor, for example, it might not work. You have a couple of options.

Learning a martial art isn't easy. Martial arts students have to push themselves. They have to learn to focus and stick with a move even when it's hard to do at first. They have to practice even when they'd rather play outside.

16    CONCENTRATION

You can give up and choose not to concentrate on making your body do the roll. But then there's no reason to be in class! You won't learn if you don't keep trying more than once.

Or you can concentrate. You can watch the teacher again. You can focus on what your arms and legs should be doing. You can try over and over again. The only thing you're thinking about is how to do the roll.

Chances are, all that concentration will pay off. You'll pay attention to yourself and get it right. After a lot of practice, you'll be able to do that roll perfectly. And along the way, you'll have practiced concentration.

## Two-Way Street

Martial arts are a good way to **improve** your concentration. But concentration also helps you get better at martial arts. It's a two-way street!

Your teacher will probably have you do exercises that improve your concentration. Before you even start moving around, you start learning about concentration.

And every time you're practicing martial arts, you're practicing concentration. Then you can use your new concentration skills in other parts of your life, like at school.

But you'll also get better at martial arts. When you concentrate, you get better at doing all the moves your teacher is showing you. Without concentration, getting better at martial arts may take a lot of time. But with concentration, you'll soon be moving up to higher levels!

# 3

# IMPROVING YOUR CONCENTRATION

**P**eople can't just concentrate all the time without practice. Some of us are better at concentrating than others. Concentrating can be really tough for others. But that doesn't mean we can't all learn how to concentrate better. It's something you can get better at if you want to.

Martial arts are one way to improve your concentration. There are other ways, too. Not everyone wants to practice martial arts. Or they want extra practice concentrating. Everyone can concentrate better if they follow a few tips.

## Eating for Concentration

You don't have to sit in class and learn how to concentrate. You might get bored. And then you won't be able to concentrate. That's the opposite of what you want!

Playing games can be a great way to learn concentration. A game like checkers takes some quick thinking and smart choices. Plus, you have to learn and remember the rules to the game.

You can do lots of other things to improve your concentration. One is changing what you eat.

When you eat a lot of sugar, what happens? You might get a lot of energy all at once. Then you crash and get really tired.

Sugar isn't good for concentrating. At first, you have too much energy to concentrate on something like homework. You want to run around as much as you can and use up all that energy. Then you don't have enough energy, and you would rather just sleep or watch TV. You don't want to concentrate on something.

If you want to feel better and be able to concentrate, skip the sugar. That doesn't mean you can't ever eat sugar. But save eating lots of cookies and candy for special days.

Lots of foods have sugar in them. Soda, sweet cereal, and some kinds of yogurt all have lots and lots of sugar. Try eating less of these foods and see what happens.

If you still want sugar, eat some fruit. Eating more fruits and vegetables will help you concentrate. They'll make your body and brain work better. You'll have

more energy for your school day. And that will help you focus on what you're learning and doing.

# Sleep

Many people don't get enough sleep. They stay up late watching TV. They don't go to bed early enough. Or they have to get up really early for work or school.

But getting enough sleep is one of the easiest ways we can be healthier. And concentration is a lot easier with a good night's sleep.

Maybe you can remember a night you didn't get enough sleep. Did you have anything important to do the next day? What if you had to play in a soccer game or take a test? How did you feel? Could you pay attention to what was going on?

Probably not. Instead, you might have wanted to crawl back into bed. Focusing on the soccer game or test was a lot tougher without a good night's sleep. You probably didn't do as well. You might have had a lot of trouble concentrating. All because you didn't get enough sleep.

Most people need about eight hours of sleep a night. Kids often need a little more, around nine or ten hours. Our bodies and brains rest during sleep. They rest for another day of hard work. If we don't get enough sleep, we just don't do things as well as we could. We're not ready for the day.

So try getting eight or nine hours of sleep every night, at least. Go to bed at the same time every night. Get up at the same time in the morning. You'll feel better. And you'll be able to concentrate better!

# Games

Getting better at concentrating doesn't have to be hard or a chore. You can make it fun! Playing games can improve your concentration just like eating better and sleeping more.

Games make you focus on something for a while. You have to concentrate really hard on the game in front of you if you want to win.

Any board game or card game will work. Memory games are good at helping you practice concentration. There's no way to win a memory game unless you really concentrate on remembering.

All martial arts students must remember the moves they learn in class. Students have to practice the moves again and again until they get them right. It takes a lot to learn martial arts, but that kind of focus can help make your life better.

## Memorizing in Karate

In karate, students learn kata. Kata are a bunch of steps done in a specific order. Students have to memorize kata and then do them right. In karate, kata are usually done by just one person. (In other kinds of martial arts, two people might do one kata together.) There are lots and lots of different kata to learn in karate. Each kata involves steps, twists, kicks, punches, and more. And each kata has lots of steps. Students need concentration to memorize the steps and do them in order. That's one of the main ways students learn concentration in karate.

CONCENTRATION

Puzzles are also good at helping you concentrate. They can be jigsaw puzzles, crosswords, Sudoku, or anything else. You have to be focused and you have to be patient. You have to concentrate to solve them. The more you practice concentrating, the better you'll be. It's like practicing an instrument or a sport. The more you do it, the better you'll get.

# Practicing in Martial Arts

Your martial arts teacher will help you practice concentrating. Before you learn all the fancy moves, your master will teach you how to relax and concentrate.

You might even do some **meditation** in class. Meditation is focusing on one thing to relax. That one thing could be a sound, or word, or your breathing. It forces you to concentrate on just one thing. Nothing else is distracting you.

Meditation helps you to feel calm. It helps you focus on what is going on right now. A lot of the time, you might be thinking about the test that's coming up tomorrow. Or the fight you had with your parents. Meditation helps you stop worrying about all that. You can't concentrate if you're worried. So meditation helps you concentrate.

Martial arts help you concentrate in other ways too. In martial arts, there are lots of things you have to memorize. Memorizing takes concentration.

In many forms of martial arts, you have to learn a few words in another language like Japanese or Korean. Each move has a name in a different language. You have to know which move is which to keep up in class. So, you have to memorize all these new words. You might also have to memorize numbers in another language.

There are also times when you have to do many moves in a row. You need to memorize in which order the moves go. The only way to do that is to concentrate on what the teacher is doing. Then you have to concentrate on what you're doing. You have to focus on remembering each step in order. It's hard! But it's worth it.

# 4

# CONCENTRATION AND YOUR LIFE

Concentration is a skill we all need. If we couldn't concentrate, we couldn't get anything done. Focusing on the important things we have to do helps us to do them well.

Think about your day. When do you concentrate? You concentrate a little when you get dressed and brush your teeth. You don't stop thinking about brushing your teeth in the middle. You focus on finishing the task. Later, you concentrate on your teacher at school. You might have to concentrate on writing for a little while. Or on reading from a book. During free time, you concentrate on playing a game with your friends. You have to focus on the rules and on winning. Those are just a few of the times you use concentration every day.

Martial arts teach you skills you can use every day. You might not use your chopping and kicking skills much outside of martial arts. But you will use the concentration you learn.

# Kung Fu Breathing

In kung fu, students learn how to concentrate on breathing. It's called meditation. Lots of martial arts use meditation, not just kung fu. In class, your teacher will tell you to only think about breathing. He or she will tell you to think about how you're breathing in and out. You'll be focusing a lot on just breathing. It helps calm you down. It also lets you focus and make your kung fu moves better. Meditation is a good way to stay focused. If you can't concentrate at school or somewhere else, try just thinking about breathing. It might help you to stay focused on what's in front of you.

# In School

Concentration will help you do better in school. School is all about concentrating. You have to focus on the teacher when he's talking. You have to focus on tests when you're studying or taking them. You have to focus on doing homework.

Lots of kids have trouble concentrating. It's hard to pay attention to school if you'd rather be playing on the playground or playing computer games!

But paying attention in school is important. And if you practice martial arts, you will know how to pay attention.

Once you get better at concentrating at school, a lot of things happen. You start doing all your homework because you can focus on finishing it. You'll be patient enough to read the books you're meant to read. You can concentrate on tests when you're taking them.

All that means you'll get better grades. When you finish your homework and pay attention to tests, you get better grades. And you learn more! That's the point of school, after all.

You might even get in less trouble. If your teacher is always yelling at you for daydreaming in class, martial arts could help fix your problems. Instead of staring into space or falling asleep, you'll be able to pay attention. Your teacher will be happy, and you'll be happy too.

## Martial Arts and ADHD

Some scientists have found that martial arts even help kids with attention-deficit hyperactivity disorder (ADHD). Kids with ADHD have trouble paying attention. They need to move around a lot. Martial arts can help them focus. It isn't a magic cure, but it does teach kids with ADHD how to concentrate. It also helps them get rid of extra energy. Scientists have learned that martial arts are even more helpful than other kinds of exercise for kids with ADHD.

# Sports

Martial arts can help you be better at sports, too. Maybe you play soccer or basketball or another sport. You have to concentrate on sports, just like martial arts.

You need concentration to score goals. If you can't focus on where the goal is and where the rest of your teammates are, chances are you won't score many goals. You have to put your whole attention on the game you're playing.

In sports, you're moving your body just like you do in martial arts. You probably use different movements, but it's the same idea. Focusing on what your body is doing will help you get better at your sport.

# Art

Maybe you dance or play an instrument. Or you paint or make things out of clay. Focus and patience are important for working on art or music.

You need to concentrate on the notes and the conductor when you're playing in an orchestra. You have to focus on making your drawing look like a horse or a dragon. If you can't concentrate, you might just give up. You can't pay enough attention to finish what you're doing.

To play well in band or finish that drawing, you have to concentrate. Martial arts can give you the concentration skills you need.

# Friends and Family

Concentration is for more than just tests and sports. Concentration makes your relationships better. You have a relationship with your parents. And with your siblings and cousins. And with your friends. Anytime we are connected to someone, we call it a relationship.

Do you ever pay attention to what other people are feeling? Do you notice if your friend gets upset at something you do? Do you know how to make someone feel better? Your friends and family will like it if you pay attention to their feelings. Martial arts can actually help you with all that.

Concentrating on relationships means paying attention to other people. It's about thinking of what other people are feeling. A lot of us don't think much about other people's feelings. We think more about our own.

But by learning how to concentrate, you notice more things in life. You notice if your friend is thankful you helped her out on some homework. You notice if your brother gets upset because you said something mean to him. And when you notice, you can fix things you did wrong. And you can remember to do nice things.

# It Doesn't End There

Martial arts can help you out a lot. You learn how to defend yourself. You learn how to move in new ways. And you also learn important life skills like concentration.

Martial arts aren't the only way to learn how to focus better, but they're a great way to improve your concentration. Take what you learn in martial arts and use it in everyday life! It's a tool you can use all the time.

# Words to know

**defend:** Keep others from hurting you.

**distracted:** Having a hard time focusing or having your attention drawn to something other than what you're doing.

**improve:** To get better at.

**meditation:** A calming time of focusing on your breathing to clear your mind and relax.

**practice:** To learn, use, and train to become better.

**respect:** Treating others the way you want to be treated. This can mean listening to your teachers and friends or thinking of others' feelings.

**skills:** Things you learn that help you become a better person or live a better life.

**traditions:** Ways of doing things that have been used for many years.

# Find Out More

## ONLINE

Kidz World: Karate
www.kidzworld.com/article/4918-martial-arts-karate

Martial Arts History Museum
martialartsmuseum.com

PBS Kids
pbskids.org/itsmylife/body/solosports/article2.html

## IN BOOKS

Goodman, Didi. *The Kids' Karate Workbook: A Take-Home Training Guide for Young Martial Artists*. Berkeley, Cal.: Blue Snake Books, 2009.

Park, Y.H. *Taekwondo for Kids*. Boston: Tuttle Publishing, 2005.

Scandiffio, Laura. *The Martial Arts Book*. Toronto, Ont.: Annick Press, 2010.

# Index

attention-deficit and hyperactivity
disorder (ADHD) 27

capoeira 9

exercise 10, 17, 27

fighting 7, 9

games 11, 20, 21, 26
grades 11, 26

homework 11, 26, 28

jiu-jitsu 8

karate 8, 22

master 7, 13, 15, 23
meditation 23, 26

practice 9–10, 15–17, 19, 21 23, 27

relationships 28

school 7, 10–11, 15, 17, 21, 25, 26
sleep 20–21, 26
sports 11, 27, 28
sugar 20

taekwondo 8–9, 15
teacher 9, 11, 13–17, 23, 26

# About the Author

Kim Etingoff lives in Boston, Massachusetts, spending part of her time working on farms. Kim writes educational books for young people on topics including health, nutrition, and more.

# Picture Credits

www.Dreamstime.com
    Dragang: p. 16
    Dragang: p. 6
    Joeygil: p. 14
    Joeygil: p. 22
    Mamahoohooba: p. 24
    Mvogel: p. 8
    Poco_bw: p. 12
    Sleiselei: p. 18
    Sonyae: p. 20